blur

The Chord Songbook

Wise Publications
London/New York/Paris/Sydney/Copenhagen/Madrid

Exclusive Distributors
Music Sales Limited
8/9 Frith Street,
London W1V 5TZ, England.
Music Sales Pty Limited
120 Rothschild Avenue,
Rosebery, NSW 2018, Australia.

Order No. AM936914
ISBN 0-7119-5736-3
This book © Copyright 1996 by Wise Publications

Compiled by Peter Evans
Music arranged by Howard Johnstone
Music processed by The Pitts

Cover design by Pearce Marchbank, Studio Twenty
Quarked by Ben May
Cover photograph by All Action

Printed in the United Kingdom by
Caligraving Limited, Thetford, Norfolk.

Your Guarantee of Quality
As publishers, we strive to produce every book
to the highest commercial standards.
This book has been carefully designed to minimise awkward
page turns and to make playing from it a real pleasure.
Particular care has been given to specifying acid-free,
neutral-sized paper made from pulps which have not been
elemental chlorine bleached. This pulp is from farmed sustainable
forests and was produced with special regard for the environment.
Throughout, the printing and binding have been planned to
ensure a sturdy, attractive publication which should give years
of enjoyment. If your copy fails to meet our high standards,
please inform us and we will gladly replace it.

Music Sales' complete catalogue describes thousands
of titles and is available in full colour sections by subject,
direct from Music Sales Limited. Please state your areas of interest
and send a cheque/postal order for £1.50 for postage to:
Music Sales Limited, Newmarket Road,
Bury St. Edmunds, Suffolk IP33 3YB.

Relative Tuning

The guitar can be tuned with the aid of pitch pipes or dedicated electronic guitar tuners which are available through your local music dealer. If you do not have a tuning device, you can use relative tuning. Estimate the pitch of the 6th string as near as possible to E or at least a comfortable pitch (not too high, as you might break other strings in tuning up). Then, while checking the various positions on the diagram, place a finger from your left hand on the:

5th fret of the E or 6th string and **tune the open A** (or 5th string) to the note (A)

5th fret of the A or 5th string and **tune the open D** (or 4th string) to the note (D)

5th fret of the D or 4th string and **tune the open G** (or 3rd string) to the note (G)

4th fret of the G or 3rd string and **tune the open B** (or 2nd string) to the note (B)

5th fret of the B or 2nd string and **tune the open E** (or 1st string) to the note (E)

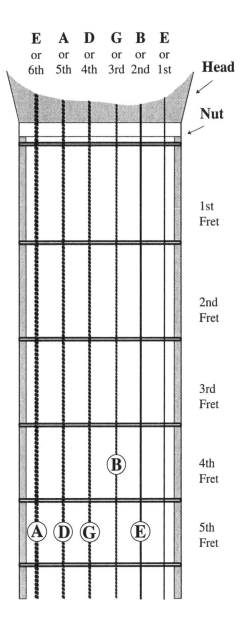

Reading Chord Boxes

Chord boxes are diagrams of the guitar neck viewed head upwards, face on as illustrated. The top horizontal line is the nut, unless a higher fret number is indicated, the others are the frets.

The vertical lines are the strings, starting from E (or 6th) on the left to E (or 1st) on the right.

The black dots indicate where to place your fingers.

Strings marked with an O are played open, not fretted.

Strings marked with an X should not be played.

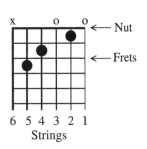

3

Badhead

Words & Music by
Damon Albarn, Graham Coxon, Alex James and David Rowntree

Am   D   C   A   G   C/G   B♭6   Em

Intro

| Am | D | C | A ‖

| G | C/G | G | C/G |

Verse 1

G   C/G   G
So far I've not really stayed in touch,
C/G   B♭6   C
Well you knew as much, it's no surprise
        G   C/G   G
That today I'll get up around two,
C/G   B♭6   C
From a lack of anything to do.

Chorus 1

         Am   D
And I might as well just grin and bear it,
          C   A
'Cause it's not worth the trouble of an argument.

Verse 2

       G   C/G   G
And you've not really stayed in touch,
C/G   B♭6   C
Well I knew as much, it's no surprise
        G   C/G   G
That today I'll get up around two,
C/G   B♭6   C
With nothing to do except get a touch of 'flu.

Chorus 2

         Am   D
And I might as well just grin and bear it,
          C   A
'Cause it's not worth the trouble of an argument,
         Am   D
And in any case I'd rather wear it,
          C   A
It's like a bad head in the morning.

Instrumental | **Am Em** | **Am** | **Am Em** | **C** | **C** **D** ‖

Instrumental Chords as Verse 1

Instrumental Chords as Chorus 2

Chorus 3
        Am   **D**
And I might as well just grin and bear it,
            C   **A**
'Cause it's not worth the trouble of an argument,
        Am   **D**
And in any case I'd rather wear it,
            C   **A**
It's like a bad head in the morning.

Chorus 4 As Chorus 3

Instrumental | **Am Em** | **Am** | **Am Em** | **C** | **C** **D** | **G** ‖

Best Days

Words & Music by
Damon Albarn, Graham Coxon, Alex James and David Rowntree

C   G   A♭   F   Am

Dm   Dm/C   C/B   Am⁷   A♭/G

Intro   ‖: C   G | A♭   F   :‖

Verse 1

    C   Am   C
Bow bells say goodbye to the last train,
            Am   Dm
Over the river they all go again,
            Dm/C G
Out into the leafy nowhere,
Dm   Dm/C F   G
Hope someone's waiting out there for them.
C   Am   C
Cabbie has his mind on a fare to the sun,
            Am   Dm
He works nights but it's not much fun,
            Dm/C G
Picks up the London yoyos,
Dm   Dm/C   F   G
All on their own down Soho, take me home.

Chorus 1

C   C/B   Am⁷
Other people wouldn't like to hear you
A♭   A♭/G   F   A♭   G
If you said that these are the best days of our lives.
C   C/B   Am⁷
Other people turn around and laugh at you
A♭   A♭/G   F   A♭ G C   G
If you said that these are the best days of our lives.

Instrumental | A♭   F | C | Am | C | Am |

Middle

```
Dm      Dm/C        G
Trellick Tower's been calling,
  Dm        Dm/C          F        G
I know she'll leave me in the morning.
```

Verse 2

```
        C         Am           C
In hotel cells, listening to dial tones,
        Am                 Dm
Remote controls and cable moans,
       Dm/C    G
In his drink he's talking,
Dm          Dm/C  F                   G
Gets disconnected sleep walking back home.
```

Chorus 2

```
   C           C/B         Am⁷
Other people wouldn't like to hear you
A♭      A♭/G          F       A♭    G
If you said that these are the best days of our lives.
   C           C/B         Am⁷
Other people turn around and laugh at you
A♭      A♭/G          F       A♭ G C    G
If you said that these are the best days of our lives.
A♭  F    C
   Of our lives.
```

Piano solo

```
| Am      | C      | Am      | Dm    Dm/C |
| G       | Dm  Dm/C | F      | G          |
```

Chorus 3

```
   C           C/B         Am⁷
Other people wouldn't like to hear you
A♭      A♭/G          F       A♭    G
If you said that these are the best days of our lives.
   C           C/B         Am⁷
Other people turn around and laugh at you
A♭      A♭/G          F       A♭    G
If you said that these are the best days of our lives.
```

Chorus 4

```
   C           C/B         Am⁷
Other people break into a cold sweat
A♭      A♭/G          F       A♭    G
If you said that these are the best days of their lives.
   C           C/B         Am⁷
Other people turn around and laugh at you
A♭      A♭/G          F       A♭ G C
If you said that these are the best days of our lives.
A♭ G  C    A♭ G  C
Of our lives.
```

Charmless Man

Words & Music by
Damon Albarn, Graham Coxon, Alex James and David Rowntree

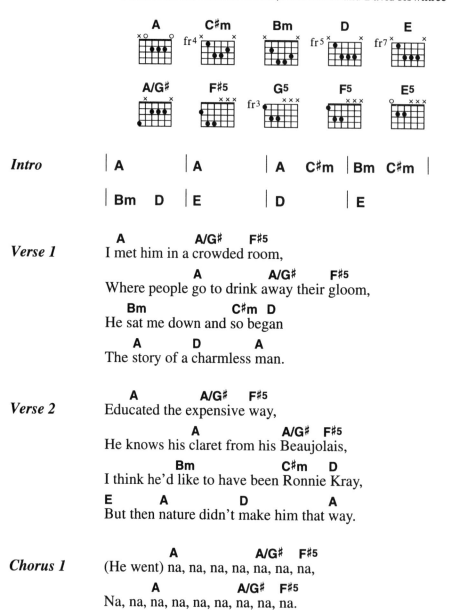

Intro

| A | A | A C#m | Bm C#m |

| Bm D | E | D | E |

Verse 1

A   A/G#   F#5
I met him in a crowded room,

A   A/G#   F#5
Where people go to drink away their gloom,

Bm   C#m D
He sat me down and so began

A   D   A
The story of a charmless man.

Verse 2

A   A/G#   F#5
Educated the expensive way,

A   A/G#   F#5
He knows his claret from his Beaujolais,

Bm   C#m   D
I think he'd like to have been Ronnie Kray,

E   A   D   A
But then nature didn't make him that way.

Chorus 1

A   A/G#   F#5
(He went) na, na, na, na, na, na, na,

A   A/G#   F#5
Na, na, na, na, na, na, na, na, na.

Bridge 1

          A
He thinks his educated airs, those family shares

C♯m   **Bm**   **C♯m**   **Bm**
Will protect him, that we'll respect him.

        E   **A**
He moves in circles of friends

            C♯m   **Bm**
Who just pretend that they like him.

   C♯m   **Bm**   **D**
He does the same to them,

           E
And when you put it all together

        D   **A**
There's the model of a charmless man.

Chorus 2

A   **A/G♯**   **F♯5**
Na, na, na, na, na, na, na,

      A   **A/G♯**   **F♯5**
Na, na, na, na, na, na, na, na, na.

Verse 3

        A   **A/G♯** **F♯5**
He knows the swingers and their cavalry,

       A   **A/G♯**   **F♯5**
Says he can get in anywhere for free.

 Bm   **C♯m**   **D**
I began to go a little cross-eyed,

        A   **D**   **A**
And from this charmless man I just had to hide.

Chorus 3

A   **A/G♯**   **F♯5**
Na, na, na, na, na, na, na,

      A   **A/G♯**   **F♯5**
Na, na, na, na, na, na, na, na, na.

Bridge 2

        A
He talks at speed, he gets nose bleeds,

         C♯m   **Bm**   **C♯m**   **Bm**
He doesn't see his days are tumbling down upon him,

   E   **A**
And yet he tries so hard to please,

         C♯m   **Bm**
He's just so keen for you to listen,

   C♯m   **Bm**   **D**
But no one is listening.

          E
And when you put it all together

        D   **A**
There's the model of a charmless man.

Instrumental   Chords as Verse 1

Bridge 3
              A
He thinks his educated airs, those family shares

C♯m   Bm   **C♯m   Bm**
Will protect him, that you'll respect him.

        E   **A**
And yet he tries so hard to please,

               C♯m Bm
He's just so keen for you to listen,

      C♯m   **Bm**   **D**
But no one is listening.

              E
And when you put it all together

        D   **A**
There's the model of a charmless man.

Chorus 4
A   **A/G♯ F♯5**
Na, na, na, na, na, na, na,

       A   **A/G♯**   **F♯5**
Na, na, na, na, na, na, na, na, na.

       A   **A/G♯**   **F♯5**
Na, na, na, na, na, na, na, na, na,

       A   **A/G♯**
Na, na, na, na, na, na, na, na,

G5   **F♯5**
Na, na, na, na, na, na,

F5   **E5**   **A**
Na, na, na, na, na, na, na.

Country House

Words & Music by
Damon Albarn, Graham Coxon, Alex James and David Rowntree

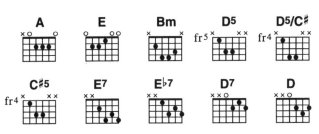

Intro

| A | E | Bm | Bm |

| D5 | D5/C♯ | C♯5 | C♯5 |

Spoken   So the story begins.

Verse 1

A
City dweller,

   E
Successful feller,

Bm
Thought to himself, "Oops,

I've got a lot of money,

D5   D5/C♯   C♯5
Caught in a rat race terminally,

         A
I'm a professional cynic

     E
But my heart's not in it,

   Bm
I'm paying the price of living life at the limit,

D5   D5/C♯   C♯5
Caught up in the century's anxiety".

     E
Yes, it preys on him,

He's getting thin.

Chorus 1

                 A   **E⁷**   **E♭⁷** **D⁷**

Now he lives in a house, a very big house in the country,

Watching afternoon repeats

                        A

And the food that he eats in the country.

He takes all manner of pills

                     E⁷   **E♭⁷** **D⁷**

And piles up analyst's bills in the country.

Ooh, it's like an Animal Farm,

                A

Lots of rural charm in the country.

Verse 2

          A

He's got morning glory

    E

And life's a different story,

Bm

Everything's going Jackanory,

D⁵   **D⁵/C♯**   **C♯⁵**

In touch with his own mortality.

        A   **E**

He's reading Balzac, knocking back Prozac,

       Bm   **D⁵**

It's a helping hand that makes you feel wonderfully bland,

            D⁵/C♯   **C♯⁵**

Oh, it's the century's remedy

        E

For the faint of heart, a new start.

Chorus 2

         A   **E⁷**   **E♭⁷** **D⁷**

He lives in a house, a very big house in the country,

He's got a frog in his chest

                     A

So he needs a lot of rest in the country.

He doesn't drink, smoke, laugh,

                   E⁷   **E♭⁷** **D⁷**

Takes herbal baths in the country,

But you'll come to no harm

                     A

On the Animal Farm in the country.

E
In the country,

In the country,

In the country.

Instrumental   Chords as Verse

Bridge
        A   **E**
Blow, blow me out
         D
I am so sad,
             A
I don't know why.
A   **E**
Blow, blow me out
         D
I am so sad,
             A
I don't know why.

Chorus 3   As Chorus 1

Chorus 4   As Chorus 2

Instrumental   Chords as Chorus   *Repeat to fade*

Dan Abnormal

Words & Music by
Damon Albarn, Graham Coxon, Alex James and David Rowntree

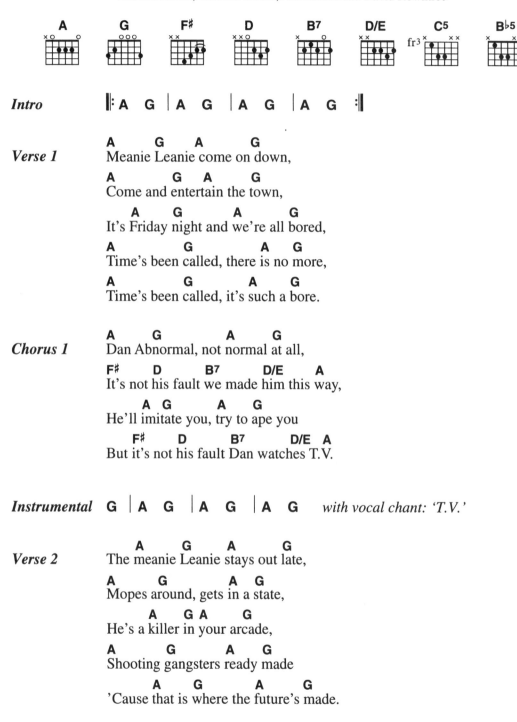

Intro   ‖: A G │ A G │ A G │ A G :‖

Verse 1

A   G   A   G
Meanie Leanie come on down,

A   G A   G
Come and entertain the town,

    A   G   A   G
It's Friday night and we're all bored,

A   G   A   G
Time's been called, there is no more,

A   G   A   G
Time's been called, it's such a bore.

Chorus 1

A   G   A   G
Dan Abnormal, not normal at all,

F♯   D   B7   D/E   A
It's not his fault we made him this way,

     A G   A   G
He'll imitate you, try to ape you

       F♯   D   B7   D/E A
But it's not his fault Dan watches T.V.

Instrumental G │ A G │ A G │ A G   *with vocal chant: 'T.V.'*

Verse 2

      A   G   A   G
The meanie Leanie stays out late,

A   G   A   G
Mopes around, gets in a state,

      A   G A   G
He's a killer in your arcade,

A   G   A   G
Shooting gangsters ready made

        A   G   A   G
'Cause that is where the future's made.

Chorus 2	As Chorus 1

Bridge ‖: **A G** | **A G** | **A G** | **A G** :‖ *with vocal chant: 'T.V.'*
and 'Teleport me'.

Middle
F♯   **D**
Dan went to his local burger bar,
                    C⁵
I want a McNormal and chips
                B♭5
Or I'll blow you to bits,
G
Give us it.

Guitar solo ‖: **A G** | **A G** | **A G** | **A G** :‖

Verse 3
                    A   G   A   G
It's the miseries at half past three,
A   G   A   G
Watching video nasties,
                A   G   A   G
He has dirty dreams when he's asleep
                A   G   A   G
'Cause Dan's just like you and me,
A   G   A   G
He's the meanie leanie. (Altogether now)

Chorus 3	As Chorus 1

Chorus 4
A   G   A   G
Dan Abnormal, not normal at all,
F♯   D   B⁷   D/E   A
It's not his fault we made him this way,
            A G   A   G
He'll imitate you, try to ape you
        F♯   D   B⁷   D/E   A
But it's not his fault Dan Abnormal's me.
G   A G   A G A   G   A
    La, la, la, la,   la, la, la, la,
G   A G   A G A   G   A
    La, la, la, la,   la, la, la, la.

15

End Of A Century

Words & Music by
Damon Albarn, Graham Coxon, Alex James and David Rowntree

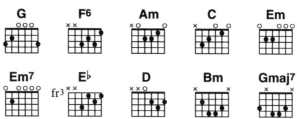

Intro | G   F⁶ | Am   C | G   F⁶ | C

Verse 1
           G   **Gmaj⁷**
She says there's ants in the carpet,
Em   **Em⁷**
Dirty little monsters,
E♭   **D**
Eating all the morsels,
Bm   **C**
Picking up the rubbish.
G   **Gmaj⁷**
Give her effervescence,
      Em   **Em⁷**
She needs a little sparkle.
E♭   **D**
Good morning, T. V.,
      Bm   **C**
You're looking so healthy.

Chorus 1
Em   **D**
We all say "Don't want to be alone",
Em   **D**
We wear the same clothes 'cause we feel the same,
Em   **D**   **C**
And kiss with dry lips when we say goodnight.
        G
End of a century,
C
Oh, it's nothing special.

Verse 2

```
      G              Gmaj7
Sex on the T.V.,

Em              Em7
Everybody's at it,

        Eb        D
And the mind gets dirty

      Bm      C
As you get closer to thirty.

      G              Gmaj7
He gives her a cuddle,

        Em              Em7
They're glowing in a huddle.

Eb          D        Bm
Good night T.V., you're all made up

C
And you're looking like me.
```

Chorus 2   As Chorus 1

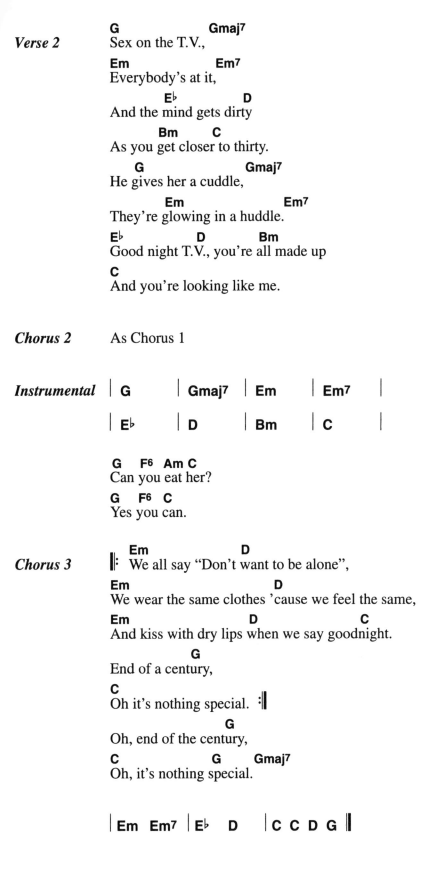

Instrumental
```
| G        | Gmaj7   | Em      | Em7      |

| Eb       | D       | Bm      | C        |
```

```
G   F6  Am  C
Can you eat her?
G   F6  C
Yes you can.
```

Chorus 3
```
      Em              D
╎: We all say "Don't want to be alone",

Em                    D
We wear the same clothes 'cause we feel the same,

Em              D           C
And kiss with dry lips when we say goodnight.

                G
End of a century,

C
Oh it's nothing special. :╎

                G
Oh, end of the century,

C          G    Gmaj7
Oh, it's nothing special.
```

```
| Em  Em7 | Eb   D    | C  C  D  G ‖
```

Ernold Same

Words & Music by
Damon Albarn, Graham Coxon, Alex James and David Rowntree

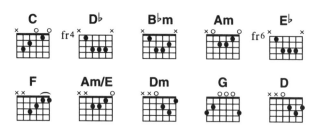

Verse 1
(spoken)

  C D♭   C
Ernold Same awoke from the same dream

B♭m   C
In the same bed at the same time.

           Am
Looked in the same mirror,

         E♭
Made the same frown

      G   C
And felt the same way as he did every day.

      D♭   C
Then Ernold Same caught the same train

       B♭m   C
At the same station, sat in the same seat

           Am
With the same nasty stain,

          E♭
Next to same old what's-his-name,

G   D♭
On his way to the same place with the same name.

(sung)

          E♭
La, la, la, la, la, la,

          D♭
La, la, la, la, la, la,

          E♭
La, la, la, la, la, la,

    D   G
La, la.

Chorus 1

    C
Oh Ernold Same,

       Am
His world stays the same,

    F   **Am/E**   **Dm**
Today will always be tomorrow.

Chorus 2

    C
Poor old Ernold Same,

      Am
He's getting that feeling again,

  F   **Am/E**   **Dm**   **G**
Nothing, nothing will change tomorrow.

  D♭   **E♭**
La, la, la, la, la, la,

           D♭
La, la, la, la, la, la,

             E♭ **D**   **G**   **C**
La, la, la, la, la, la.

Girls And Boys

Words & Music by
Damon Albarn, Graham Coxon, Alex James and David Rowntree

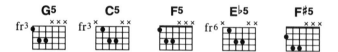

Verse 1

G5
Streets like a jungle,

C5
So call the police.

F5
Following the herd

E♭5　　**F♯5**　**F5**
Down to Greece on holiday.

G5
Love in the nineties

C5
Is paranoid.

F5
On sunny beaches

E♭5
Take your chances.

Chorus 1

F♯5　　**F5**　　**G5**
Looking for ‖: girls who are boys

Who like boys to be girls

C5
Who do boys like they're girls

Who do girls like they're boys.

F5
Always should be someone

E♭5　　**F♯5**　**F5**
You really love.　　　:‖

Instrumental　　Chords as Chorus

Verse 2

G5
Avoiding all work
       C5
'Cause there's none available.
    F5
Like battery thinkers
          E♭5   **F♯5** **F5**
Count their thoughts on 1, 2, 3, 4, 5   fingers.
G5
Nothing is wasted,
C5
Only reproduced,
    F5
You get nasty blisters.
       E♭5
Du bist sehr schön
           F♯5   **F**
But we haven't been introduced.

Chorus 2

  G5
‖: Girls who are boys who like boys
         C5
To be girls who do boys

Like they're girls who do girls

Like they're boys.
F5
Always should be someone
      E♭5   **F♯5** **F5**
You really love.   :‖

Instrumental   Chords as Chorus 2

Chorus 3   As Chorus 2

Repeat to fade

He Thought Of Cars

Words & Music by
Damon Albarn, Graham Coxon, Alex James and David Rowntree

Bm   F♯   D   C   Em   A   G♯m7   G

Verse 1

        Bm
Moscow's still red,

    F♯
The young man's dead,

D
Gone to heaven instead,

   C   **Em**   **C**   **Em**
The evening news says he was confused.

   Bm   **F♯**
The motorways will all merge soon,

    D
Lottery winner buys the moon,

      C   **Em**
They've come to save us,

     C   **Em**
The space invaders are here.

Chorus 1

            A
He thought of cars

        Em
And where to drive them,

          Bm
And who to drive them with,

         A   **F♯**
And there, there was no one, no one.

Instrumental | Bm A | G♯m7 | G | G |

                    | Bm A | G♯m7 | G | G ||

Verse 2

```
        Bm        F♯
There's panic at London Heathrow,
D                         C      Em
Everybody wants to go up into the blue,
             C       Em
But there's a ten-year queue.
       Bm        F♯
Columbia is in top gear,
       D
It shouldn't snow this time of year,
         C       Em
Now America's shot,
                 C       Em
She's gone and done the lot.
```

Chorus 2

```
                 A
He though of planes,
                      Em
And where, where to fly to,
                      Bm
And who to fly there with,
                  A      F♯
And there, there was no one, no one.
```

Instrumental

| Bm A | G♯m⁷ | G | G | |

| Bm A | G♯m⁷ | G | G | |

| C Em | C Em | C Em | A Em | Em |

Chorus 3

```
                 A
He thought of cars
             Em
And where to drive them,
                 Bm
And who to drive them with,
                  A      F♯
And there, there was no one, no one.
```

Instrumental ‖: Bm A | G♯m⁷ | G | G :‖   *Repeat to fade*

23

It Could Be You

Words & Music by
Damon Albarn, Graham Coxon, Alex James and David Rowntree

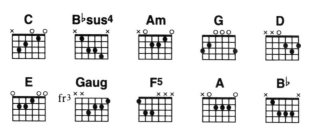

Intro   ‖: C   B♭sus4 | Am   G   :‖   *Play 4 times*

Verse 1
        C   **B♭sus4 Am**
Ch-Ch-Ch-Churchill,
  G   **D**   **E**
Got his lucky number,
           Am   **D**
Tomorrow there's another.
      G   **Gaug**
Could be me, could be you.
    C   **B♭sus4 Am**
No silver spoon,
    G   **D**   **E**
Sticky teeth they rot too soon.
          Am   **D**
You've got to have the best tunes
      G   **Gaug**
Or that's it, you've blown it.

Chorus 1
F5 E A   **D**
All we want is to be happy
F5 E A   **D**
In our homes like happy families,
F5 E C   **B♭**
Be the man on the beach
     Am   **G**
With the world at his feet.
    D   **E**
Yes, it could be you,   oh, oh oh.

Instrumental   ‖: C   B♭sus4 | Am   G   :‖

Verse 2
        C   **B♭sus4** **Am**
The likely lads

      G   **D**
Are picking up the uglies,

E   **Am**   **D**
Yesterday they were just puppies.

        G   **Gaug**
Beery slurs now life's a blur.

        C   **B♭sus4** **Am**
Telly addicts,

      G   **D** **E**
You should see them at it,

        Am **D**
Getting in a panic.

          G   **Gaug**
Will we be there, Trafalgar Square?

Chorus 2   As Chorus 1

Instrumental | **C**   **B♭** | **Am**   **G** |

       C   **B♭** **Am**   **G**
‖: Could be me,   could be you,

       C   **B♭** **Am**   **G**
  Could be me,   could be you,

       C   **B♭** **Am**   **G**
  Could be me,   could be you. :‖ **D** | **E** |

            C   **B♭sus4** **Am**
Verse 3   Well don't worry

      G   **D**   **E**
If it's not your lucky number,

                    Am   **D**
Because tomorrow there is another.

       G   **Gaug**
Could be you, could be me.

Chorus 3   As Chorus 1

      C   **B♭sus4**   **Am**   **G**
‖: Do, do do,   do, do, do. :‖ *Play 4 times*

Jubilee

Words & Music by
Damon Albarn, Graham Coxon, Alex James and David Rowntree

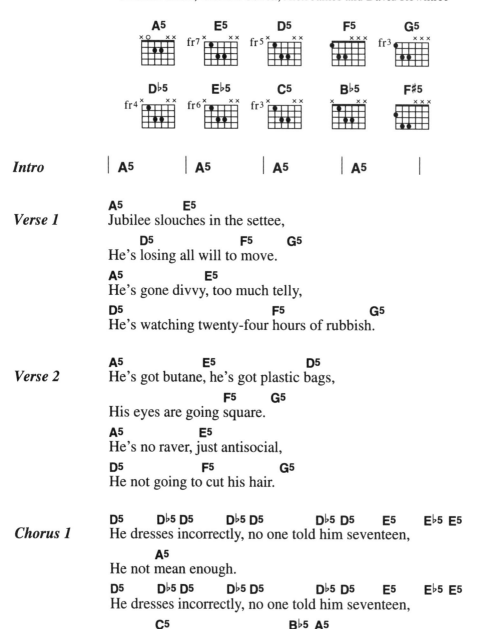

Intro | A5 | A5 | A5 | A5 |

Verse 1

A5   E5
Jubilee slouches in the settee,

        D5   F5   G5
He's losing all will to move.

A5   E5
He's gone divvy, too much telly,

D5   F5   G5
He's watching twenty-four hours of rubbish.

Verse 2

A5   E5   D5
He's got butane, he's got plastic bags,

               F5   G5
His eyes are going square.

A5   E5
He's no raver, just antisocial,

D5   F5   G5
He not going to cut his hair.

Chorus 1

D5   Db5 D5   Db5 D5   Db5 D5   E5   Eb5 E5
He dresses incorrectly, no one told him seventeen,

      A5
He not mean enough.

D5   Db5 D5   Db5 D5   Db5 D5   E5   Eb5 E5
He dresses incorrectly, no one told him seventeen,

      C5   Bb5 A5
He not keen on being like anyone else.

Verse 3

A5   **E5**
Jubilee's dad, Billy Banker,

D5   **F5** **G5**
Thinks his son's a slob.

A5   **E5**
Should get out more, stop scabbing,

D5   **F5**   **G5**
He really should go and get a job.

Chorus 2

D5   **D♭5 D5**   **D♭5 D5**   **D♭5 D5** **E5**   **E♭5 E5**
He dresses incorrectly, no one told him seventeen,

     A5
He not mean enough.

D5   **D♭5 D5**   **D♭5 D5**   **D♭5 D5**   **E5**   **E♭5 E5**
He dresses incorrectly, no one told him where to go

     A5
But he just won't get out enough.

D5   **D♭5 D5**   **D♭5 D5**   **D♭5 D5** **E5**   **E♭5 E5**
He dresses incorrectly, no one told him talk to girls

     A5
But he's just too spotty.

D5   **D♭5 D5**   **D♭5 D5**   **D♭5 D5** **E5**   **E♭5 E5**
He dresses incorrectly, no one told him seventeen,

     C5   **B♭5** **A5**
He not keen on being like anyone else,

So he just plays on his computer game.

Play 3 times

Instrumental ‖: **A5** | **A5** | **A5 F♯5** :‖ **F5** | **F5 G5** |

Chorus 3

D5   **D♭5 D5**   **D♭5 D5**   **D♭5 D5** **E5**   **E♭5 E5**
He dresses incorrectly, no one told him seventeen,

     A5
He not mean enough.

D5   **D♭5 D5**   **D♭5 D5**   **D♭5 D5**   **E5**   **E♭5 E5**
He dresses incorrectly, no one told him where to go

     A5
But he just won't get out enough.

D5   **D♭5 D5**   **D♭5 D5**   **D♭5 D5**   **E5**   **E♭5 E5**
He dresses incorrectly, no one told him talk to girls

      A5
But he's just too spotty.

D5   **D♭5 D5**   **D♭5 D5**   **D♭5 D5** **E5**   **E♭5 E5**
He dresses incorrectly, no one told him seventeen,

     C5   **B♭5**
He not keen on being like anyone.

C5   **B♭5** **C5**   **B♭5** **A5**
He's not being like anyone, Jubilee's not like anyone else.

27

Mr. Robinson's Quango

Words & Music by
Damon Albarn, Graham Coxon, Alex James and David Rowntree

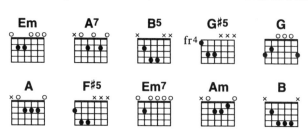

Intro | Em | A⁷ | Em | A⁷ | B⁵ | G♯⁵ | B⁵ | G♯⁵

Verse 1
               B⁵   **G♯⁵**
Oh Mister Robinson and his quango,
G
Dirty dealer, expensive car,
A
Runs the buses and the Evening Star.
            B⁵   **G♯⁵**
He got a hair piece, he got herpes,
   G
His private life is very discreet,
    A
A nicer man, no, you're never going to meet.

Bridge 1
         F♯⁵
He's the self-professed saviour of the dim right wing,

He's got respiratory problems and a mason's ring.

‖: Em Em⁷ | A Am :‖

Verse 2
               B⁵   **G♯⁵**
Oh Mister Robinson and his quango,
G
Drinks with generals and county wives,
A
The family business is doing alright.
            B⁵   **G♯⁵**
They're doing tangos down in the quangos,

G
He makes them tick, oh he makes them tock,

A
And if you don't fit he'll put you in the dock.

F#5

Bridge 2   He just sits in his leather chair and twiddles his thumbs,

Gets his secretary in and pinches her bum.

Instrumental ‖: **Em   Em7** | **A   Am** :‖ *Play 4 times*

B

Middle   He ran into the toilet in the Town Hall,

He got a biro out and he wrote on the wall:

A
"I'm wearing black French knickers under my suit,

I've got stockings and suspenders on,

I'm feeling rather loose".

F#5
Oh, I'm a naughty boy,

B5
Oh, I'm a naughty, naughty boy.

Instrumental | **G#5** | **G** | **A** | **B** | **G#5** | **G** | **A** |

Bridge 3   As Bridge 1

Instrumental ‖: **Em   Em7** | **A   Am** :‖ *Play 4 times*

F#5
‖: I'm a naughty, naughty boy. :‖ *Play 8 times*

Instrumental ‖: **F#5** | **F#5** :‖ *Repeat to fade*

Parklife

Words & Music by
Damon Albarn, Graham Coxon, Alex James and David Rowntree

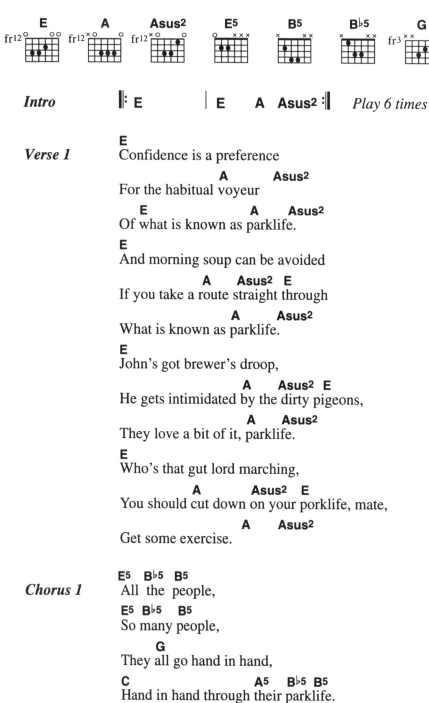

Intro   ‖: **E** | **E**   **A**   **Asus²** :‖   *Play 6 times*

Verse 1

E
Confidence is a preference

    A   **Asus²**
For the habitual voyeur

  E   **A**   **Asus²**
Of what is known as parklife.

E
And morning soup can be avoided

    A **Asus²** **E**
If you take a route straight through

    A   **Asus²**
What is known as parklife.

E
John's got brewer's droop,

    A   **Asus²** **E**
He gets intimidated by the dirty pigeons,

    A   **Asus²**
They love a bit of it, parklife.

E
Who's that gut lord marching,

   A   **Asus²** **E**
You should cut down on your porklife, mate,

    A   **Asus²**
Get some exercise.

Chorus 1

E⁵ **B♭⁵** **B⁵**
All the people,

E⁵ **B♭⁵** **B⁵**
So many people,

   G
They all go hand in hand,

C   **A⁵** **B♭⁵** **B⁵**
Hand in hand through their parklife.

Instrumental | E | E   A   Asus² | E | E   A   E |

                                    E
Verse 2   I get up when I want
                                            A
                   Except on Wednesday
                                    Asus² E   A   Asus²
                   When I get rudely awakened by the dustmen (parklife).
                                    E
                   I put my trousers on,
                                            A   Asus²
                   Have a cup of tea
                                            E   A   Asus²
                   And I think about leaving the house (parklife).
                                    E
                   I feed the pigeons,
                                            A   Asus²
                   I sometimes feed the sparrows too,
                   E   A   Asus²
                   It gives me a sense of enormous well-being (parklife),
                   E
                   And then I'm happy for the rest of the day,
                   A   Asus²   E
                   Safe in the knowledge that there will always be
                                                    A   Asus²
                   A bit of my heart devoted to it.

Chorus 2   As Chorus 1

                   E   A   Asus² E   A   Asus²
                            Parklife,   (parklife),
                   E   A   Asus² E   A   Asus²
                            Parklife,   (parklife).

                   E
                   It's got nothing to do with your
                                            A   Asus²
                   Vorsprung durch technic, you know
                   E
                   And it's not about your joggers
                                            A   Asus²
                   Who go round and round and round.

Chorus 3   As Chorus 1

                   Repeat to fade

The Universal

Words & Music by
Damon Albarn, Graham Coxon, Alex James and David Rowntree

A   **C#m**   **E**   **Bm**   **D**   **D/C#**

Intro   ‖: A   C#m | A   C#m :‖   *Play 3 times*

Verse 1
　　　　　A　　　　　　C#m　A
This is the next century
C#m　　　A　　　C#m　A
Where the universal's free,
C#m　　E　　　　Bm
You can find it anywhere,
E　　　　Bm
Yes the future's been sold.
A　　　　　　C#m　　A
Every night we're gone,
C#m　　A　　　C#m　　A
And to karaoke songs
C#m　　E　　　　　Bm
How we like to sing along,
E
'Though the words are wrong.

Chorus 1
　　　A　　　　　　　　　　　　D
It really, really, really could happen,
　　　　A　　　　　　　　　　　D
Yes it really, really, really could happen.
　　　　　　C#m
When the days they seem to fall through you,
　　　　D　　D/C#　　Bm　　E
Well just let them go.

Instrumental   ‖: A   C#m | A   C#m :‖

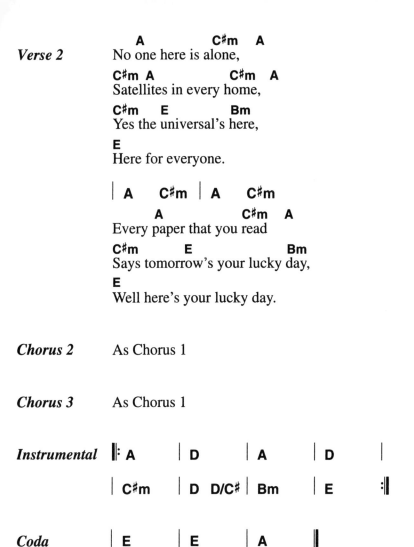

Verse 2

```
           A           C#m   A
No one here is alone,

C#m  A              C#m   A
Satellites in every home,

C#m    E          Bm
Yes the universal's here,

E
Here for everyone.


    | A    C#m | A    C#m
            A           C#m   A
Every paper that you read

C#m       E            Bm
Says tomorrow's your lucky day,

E
Well here's your lucky day.
```

Chorus 2   As Chorus 1

Chorus 3   As Chorus 1

Instrumental ‖: A | D | A | D |

                | C#m | D D/C# | Bm | E   :‖

Coda | E | E | A   ‖

This Is A Low

Words & Music by
Damon Albarn, Graham Coxon, Alex James and David Rowntree

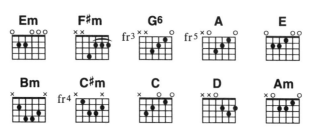

Intro | Em F#m | G6 G6—A | A | E | E

(slide)

Verse 1
          Bm   A   C#m
And into the sea goes pretty England and me,
C   Bm   E
Round the Bay of Biscay and back for tea.

                   Bm
Hit traffic on the Dogger Bank,
A   C#m
Up the Thames to find a taxi rank,
C   Bm   E
Sail on by with the tide and go to sleep.

Chorus 1
             D
This is a low
E   Am Bm
But it won't hurt you,
E   D
When you're alone
E   Am Bm
It will be there with you,
C   Bm   E
Finding ways to stay so low.

Verse 2

                   Bm
On the Tyne, Forth and Cromarty

A   **C♯m**
There's a low in the High Forties

      C   **Bm**
And Saturday's locked away on the pier,

     E
Not fast enough dear.

         Bm
And on the Malin Head

A   **C♯m**
Blackpool looks blue and red,

       C   **Bm**
And the queen she's gone round the bend,

        E
Jumped off Land's End.

Chorus 2   As Chorus 1

Instrumental | **E** | **Bm** | **A** | **C♯m** | **C** | **Bm** |

               | **E** | **E** | **E** | **Bm** | **A** | **C♯m** |

                                                    slide
               | **C** | **Bm** | **Em F♯m** | **G6** **G6 — A** | **A** ||

               E   **D**
Chorus 3 This is a low

               E   **Am Bm**
               But it won't hurt you,

               E   **D**
               When you're alone

               E   **Am Bm**
               It will be there with you.

Chorus 4   As Chorus 1

To The End

Words & Music by
Damon Albarn, Graham Coxon, Alex James and David Rowntree

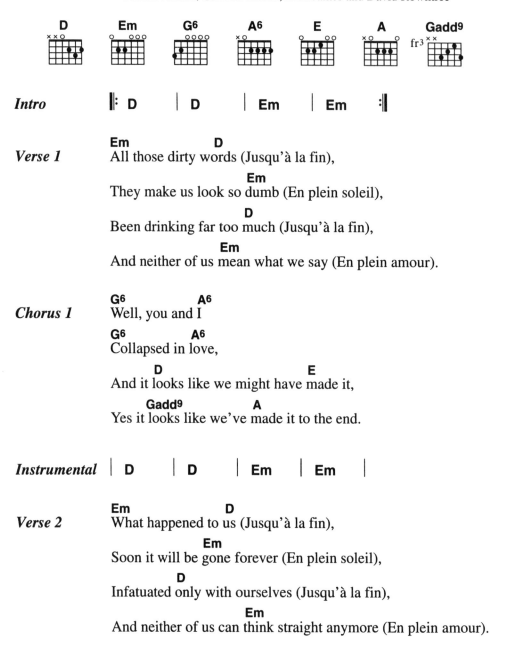

Intro ‖: D | D | Em | Em :‖

Verse 1
Em   D
All those dirty words (Jusqu'à la fin),
                     Em
They make us look so dumb (En plein soleil),
                        D
Been drinking far too much (Jusqu'à la fin),
                   Em
And neither of us mean what we say (En plein amour).

Chorus 1
G6   A6
Well, you and I
G6   A6
Collapsed in love,
          D   E
And it looks like we might have made it,
          Gadd9   A
Yes it looks like we've made it to the end.

Instrumental | D | D | Em | Em |

Verse 2
Em   D
What happened to us (Jusqu'à la fin),
                    Em
Soon it will be gone forever (En plein soleil),
               D
Infatuated only with ourselves (Jusqu'à la fin),
                     Em
And neither of us can think straight anymore (En plein amour).

Chorus 2   As Chorus 1

Chorus 3   As Chorus 1

Instrumental ‖: D | D | Em | Em   :‖   *Play 3 times*

Chorus 4   As Chorus 1

Instrumental ‖: D | D   :‖   *Repeat ad lib. to fade*

Stereotypes

Words & Music by
Damon Albarn, Graham Coxon, Alex James and David Rowntree

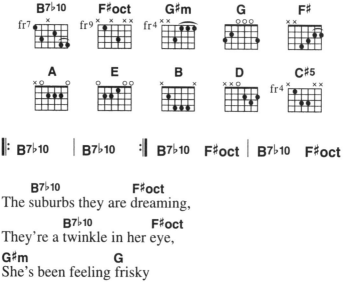

Intro ‖: B7♭10 | B7♭10 :‖ B7♭10 F♯oct | B7♭10 F♯oct

Verse 1

         B7♭10   F♯oct
The suburbs they are dreaming,

         B7♭10   F♯oct
They're a twinkle in her eye,

G♯m   G
She's been feeling frisky

         F♯
Since her husband said goodbye.

         B7♭10   F♯oct   B7♭10   F♯oct
She wears a low-cut T-shirt, runs a little B & B,

         G♯m   G   F♯
She's most accomodating when she's in her lingerie.

Bridge 1

         A
Wife swapping is your future,

You know that it would suit you.

Chorus 1

B7♭10
Yes, they're stereotypes,

There must be more to life.

G♯m   E   B
All your life you're dreaming,

         E   B
Then you stop dreaming.

         C♯5
From time to time you know

         D   E
You should be going on another bender.

Instrumental ‖: **B7♭10** **F♯oct** | **B7♭10** **F♯oct** :‖

Verse 2

      B7♭10   **F♯oct**
The suburbs they are sleeping

        B7♭10   **F♯oct**
But he's dressing up tonight,

    G♯m   **G**   **F♯**
She likes a man in uniform, he likes to wear it tight.

        B7♭10   **F♯oct**   **B7♭10**   **F♯oct**
They're on the lovers' sofa, they're on the patio,

    G♯m   **G**   **F♯**
And when the fun is over watch themselves on video.

Bridge 2

      A
The neighbours may be staring,

But they are just past caring.

Chorus 2

B7♭10
Yes, they're stereotypes,

There must be more to life.

G♯m   **E**   **B**
All your life you're dreaming,

          E   **B**
And then you stop dreaming.

     C♯5
From time to time you know

      D   **E**
You're going on another bender.

B7♭10
Yes, there must be more to life,

They're stereotypes.

Instrumental | **G♯m** | **E B** | **E B** | **E G** | **F♯** | **F♯** ‖

| **B7♭10** | **B7♭10** | **A** | **A G** | **B7♭10** | **B7♭10** |

Bridge 3

      A
Wife swapping is your future,

You know that it would suit you.

Chorus 3

B7♭10
Yes, they're stereotypes,

There must be more to life.
G♯m   **E**   **B**
All your life you're dreaming,
               E   **B**
And then you stop dreaming.
         C♯5
From time to time you know
             D   **E**
You should be going on another bender.

Chorus 4

B7♭10
Yes, there must be more to life

Than stereotypes.
G♯m   **E**   **B**
All your life you're dreaming,
               E   **B**
And then you stop dreaming.
         C♯5
From time to time you know
    D   **E**
You should be going on another bender,
F♯   **G**   **A**   **B**
Before you come to an ender.

10/00 (38375)